I0059494

STARDOM PUBLISHING

DESPERATE MARKETERS

HOW TO IDENTIFY AND AVOID UNETHICAL AND INEFFECTIVE ONLINE MARKETING STRATEGIES

RAAM ANAND

STARDOM PUBLISHING

WORLDWIDE

www.StardomPublishing.com

STARDOM PUBLISHING

A Division of Stardom Alliance
and infoYOGIS Technologies.
105-501 Silverside Road
Wilmington, DE 19809

Copyright © 2013 by Raam Anand

All rights reserved, including right to reproduce
this book or portions thereof in any form whatsoever.

First edition August 2013

Anand, Raam.

Desperate marketers: how to identify and avoid unethical and
ineffective online marketing strategies /

Raam Anand.

p. cm.

1. Marketing (Internet) I. Title

ISBN-13: 978-0615871349 (Stardom Publishing)

ISBN-10: 0615871348

Dedicated to my amazing mom and dad:
Parvathi and Ramaswamy, whom we all lovingly called
Anna and Amma, married for 50 glorious years.
We lost you both too soon,
but we carry your legacy and love, forever.

Contents

Live as if you were to die tomorrow.
Learn as if you were to live forever.

— MAHATMA GANDHI

Chapter One

Introduction
What is this book all about?

Search Engine Optimization or SEO, as it is called is DEAD. That's a bold statement and I'm going to prove this to you by sharing the proof with you in this book. And, SEO is just one part of the overall Internet marketing system. There are dozens of popular strategies that have become totally obsolete today, due to technological breakthroughs. What makes these strategies unethical is the fact that marketing consultants,

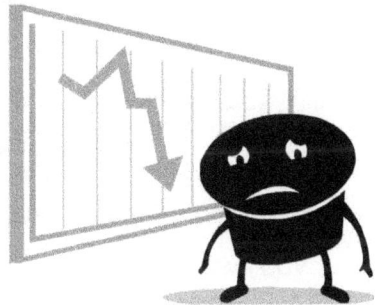

companies and agencies, trying to 'sell' these 'dead rats' to unsuspecting customers, in the name of internet marketing services and promising them great results.

Before I present you with ideas, proof, problems and solutions, here are the outcomes that you can expect from this book.

1. Pulling back the curtains.
2. Busting deep-rooted myths.
3. Finding solutions.

In this book, I'll be pulling back the curtains in the online marketing (also called as Internet marketing or SEO industry) so that you can clearly see what's happening, what's working and what's not.

I will be busting some of the deep-rooted myths in the online marketing or "SEO" world to help you understand why I consider SEO as dead. I will also show you how unscrupulous marketers and marketing companies are still using stale technology to take their clients for a royal ride.

And, this book is not just about the problems. It will also provide you the solutions to these pressing problems. This is a huge industry and every day, hundreds of thousands of people are being victimized by unethical marketing practices. This book will lay it out in front of you, help you identify unethical marketing practices and steer you away to finding other effective solutions for achieving your results.

This is not about achieving better search engine rankings or getting your keywords to the top. In fact, Google has just recently discontinued their keyword-tool, software that many SEO-Companies used to dig out keywords or phrases that people searched on Google.

This is all about finding new ways to achieve STARDOM in your industry, without getting victimized by unethical SEO or marketing perpetrators. I don't blame them because most of these so-called 'SEO' marketers don't even know that SEO is already dead. Many are perplexed because they are not able to get the 'results' they had promised to their unsuspecting clients, even though they are using all those 'proven' strategies. Some of those strategies used to work so brilliantly well, that many 'SEO' companies made millions of dollars, offering page-one rankings!

Hype, as it is known in Internet marketing parlance, is an idea that is all about a strategy or a technique that's made to appear huge and larger than life, by unscrupulous marketers. They call it the next big secret and start selling their 'secret' sauce to unsuspecting customers.

I'd consider this work as fulfilling, if it helps you understand how to identify hype from reality and staying away from unethical marketing. I would consider this work as worthwhile if it helps you achieve stardom in your chosen niche.

"Yesterday is history,
tomorrow is a mystery,
today is a gift of God,
which is why we call it the present."

— Bil Keane

Chapter Two

Why Should You Read This Book?

O kay... let me talk to you, directly. I have been below the radar for quite some time and I want to connect with you.

I started my Internet career back in the year 2001 when I started learning about Internet, marketing and sales online. Before that, the 90's, online banking was still in its infancy and most banking networks were disconnected from their ATMs, which worked independently.

I was invited by a leading bank to write programming code that could connect their banking network to their ATMs. These were two entirely different platforms. The bank network was on Unix and the ATMs were running on OS2. After 5 months of programming, the two platforms were connected and I felt like I was a super-hero!

After a decade of programming experience, I had enough of living inside a cubicle. Fast forward to 2001, I had started dreaming about becoming an entrepreneur. I devoted the next two years to learn everything I could about the Internet, search engines, marketing, sales, online advertising and every topic that I could lay my hands on.

Coming from the programming background helped me to a great extent. I was able to learn more in less time. Programming is all about organizing, discipline and precision. I applied these principles in organizing my thoughts.

My Darling

By 2004, I was ready to launch my own software programs for the Internet Marketing industry. I had transformed into a marketer. After successfully launching several software programs and information products, I started my own Internet Marketing Agency, my flagship company that I called "infoYOGIS" in the year 2006. This was my darling. My baby. I started this company to help me market my products as well as help others with their online marketing campaigns.

infoYOGIS was a one-man organization when it began. Soon, we had more campaigns to handle, more customers to serve. The hiring and training process was started. infoYOGIS started growing... from 1 to 6 people to 10 full-time employees within a year.

We started serving clients from all over the world. Our business diversified into providing SEO, Social Media and Internet Marketing services to clients and customers from all the five inhabited continents of the world.

During the next few years, infoYOGIS grew by leaps and bounds. Went from 10 employees to over 100 in 3 years. infoYOGIS was the most sought after name for SEO and Internet Marketing fulfilment. By 2011, infoYOGIS was the LARGEST Internet Marketing Agency in Asia. And, I am proud to say that I founded infoYOGIS.

Hundreds of other marketers, self-proclaimed "Guru's", SEO Companies and Marketing Agencies became our partners. We started fulfilling for our partners as their "white-label" service providers. In other words, we did all the work and they built their business around our infrastructure.

Thousands of clients came in and we, at infoYOGIS, setup a dedicated team of 5 marketing scientists, as our R&D department. Their job involved researching online marketing, advertising, search engines and other techniques. Anyone who has involved with infoYOGIS as a client, partner or service provider will know the kind of importance we give to quality, results and perfection.

Rise and fall

In fact, our successes lead thousands of other people to start their own Internet Marketing agency business. Today, there are probably tens of thousands of SEO companies all over the world. Everybody and their dog started offering SEO services, whether they knew anything about the topic.

Largely, the SEO industry was totally dependent on search engines and mainly, Google. The essence of SEO was typically getting first page ranking for selected keywords for any given website. So, unscrupulous and untrained SEO consultants and marketers started offering 'packaged' SEO and online marketing services without qualifying their prospects.

Ethics were thrown out of the window and promises were made to unsuspecting clients that could not be fulfilled. Google started releasing a series of updates to their algorithms. These 'algos' as they are popularly known as, are complex rules and conditions that match websites with their rankings when people search for specific terms on Google.

Google keeps these algos secret and they do not disclose how websites are ranked or how the algos work. Nobody knows because it is reported that Google has multiple teams working on different algos that work independently to produce the results.

Indirectly, Google started stamping out the efforts by SEO companies and rocked the boat. Well, it was not just rocking the boat. It sent a tsunami of waves that hit almost all SEO companies. Millions of website that used to rank well were thrown out of the search indices overnight, rendering all the 'hard work' that SEO companies did for their clients, useless. Top ranking websites for highly competitive keywords couldn't even be located on the search engines. Google called these events as "algorithm updates" and they after funny names likes 'panda update', 'penguin update' and so on.

Essentially, Google busted the SEO industry and over-turned all the established and 'proven' strategies in no time. It's not their fault. It is their policy. Nobody wants someone else to manipulate their methodologies for commercial gain.

Survival mode

Unfortunately, by this time, the SEO industry had grown big, huge and spread all over the world. They couldn't believe that their strategies were made worthless in a jiffy. They didn't let their customers know about this. They kept their funnels open, leading to a worldwide spread of marketing 'hype'. Suddenly everybody had a secret, weapon, strategy or a plan that worked so well and beat the 'algo-team' that Google spends millions of dollars to create and manage. A team of highly qualified engineers, scientists and researchers, some of them with multiple PhDs.

In order to stay in business, many of these small 'SEO' companies, consultants, marketers and even several established 'Gurus' chose unethical marketing practices and invented "NEW" secrets, leading to a lot of hype in the industry.

Our research and development (R&D) team had clearly established that this industry was changing rapidly and many proven online marketing strategies were no long effective. We realized that old-world strategies are not going to work in the new world. In fact, we had to terminate our contracts with several SEO Gurus and IM Consultants because the 'packages' they were selling (and we were fulfilling for them) weren't working. The strategies were no good but they had a bunch of clients that kept paying them monthly fees for SEO activities that they didn't want to stop coming in. However, I thought it was not ethical to accept money for work that wasn't helping. We had come up with other plans but change, even if it is for good, is uncomfortable.

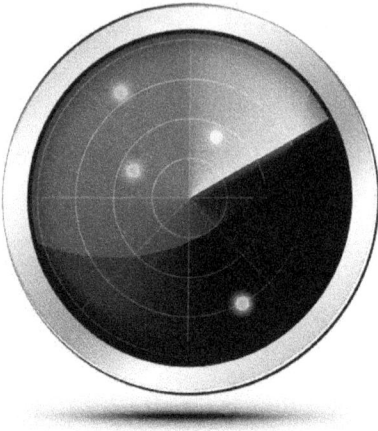

We, at infoYOGIS, started working on alternatives to SEO during the late 2011 and early 2012. There's an interesting story I share on stages and on some of my webinars/hangouts, on how all this began and how we had a big transformation. I founded an Internet Marketing Agency, took it from a 1-man operation to a 100+ people organization, serving clients from all over the world. We developed new strategies that we applied on our loyal and elite clients that made them SUPERSTARS in their niche... and all this WITHOUT depending on search engines or any other 'outside' technology. Since then, my focus is on helping my audience understand and achieve STARDOM in their niches.

In the next chapter, I am going to introduce you to some popular 'HYPE' models that are making rounds in the market today and how to avoid them. I sincerely hope that an educated market will help cleanse the industry and stop unsuspecting customers from getting ripped off by unethical marketing companies and unscrupulous consultants.

Don't lower your expectations to meet your performance.
Raise your level of performance to meet your expectations.
Expect the best of yourself, and then do what is necessary
to make it a reality.

— Ralph Marston

Chapter Three

Hype And Reality
The Good.. The Bad.. and The Ugly..

Here's the definition of the word "hype" from the Merriam-Webster dictionary:

hype /hīp/

Noun

1. Extravagant or intensive publicity or promotion.
2. A hypodermic needle or injection.

Verb

1. Promote or publicize (a product or idea) intensively, often exaggerating its importance or benefits.
2. Stimulate or excite (someone): "I was hyped up because I wanted to do well".

If you have been on the Internet for some time, I'm sure you have seen a lot of 'hype' going around. This is especially easy spot in the information and marketing industry.

Tricky marketers use several mechanisms and methods to create 'hype'. In fact, there are even courses and seminars that teach people how to create 'hype' disguised as marketing strategies. Some of these courses became highly popular and helped their creators' make millions of dollars in sales within a few days of their launch. Hype helped make money! But, not all those who purchased the product were able to replicate the same success. That's a different story.

Let's begin by identifying some of the most popular hypes that are making rounds.

SCARCITY

In her article titled "How Scarcity Leads to Spending" in the TIME magazine, Maia Szalavitz explains how economic uncertainty and exposure to scarcity makes people to spend more and risk more. This article was based on a research report published in Psychological Science magazine, to help explain why poverty can sometimes be so difficult to escape.

Scarcity is psychological trigger that unethical marketers use to influence their prospects to buy from them. This is very much prevalent in online marketing industry and it is one of the reasons for many successful product-launches online.

The basic definition of scarcity is "having fewer resources than needed to fill human wants and needs."

There are indeed certain resources that are scarce. In this context, for example, time is a limited resource. If someone is trading their time, then they can say it is scarce because there is only a limited availability of 'time'. On the other, you see many "online programs", information products, eBooks, home-study courses and even seminars, using the scarcity trick.

eBooks can be sold unlimited number of times. Online training program can accommodate thousands of participants to log in and use the training at the same time. Today's technology has developed so well that it can support hundreds of thousands of people across the world to access information seamlessly.

Some marketers apply the scarcity principle even to online broadcast events like webinars. Only 200 people can participate. Open only for the first 500 people who login in. All this is nonsense. Today, using Google Hangout, anyone can broadcast their webinar or event, LIVE to virtually unlimited number of people all over the world. The technology is so developed and inexpensive that anyone can practically do LIVE broadcast of any event with just a computer and an Internet connection.

So, when you see this scarcity tactic in any promotional material that you come across, pause for a moment and think whether the offer is really scarce that you need to act immediately.

DISCOUNTS

This is another tactic that creates a lot of hype and urgency to buy from unsuspecting prospects.

Discount is a psychological hot button that marketers have effective used over centuries to make people buy their stuff right now, instead of thinking about it later.

By offering discounts, marketers sell more stuff in less time. This tactic is extremely good for… well, marketers. It puts more money into their pockets.

Discounts only make sense when the item offered has been sold or will surely be sold at a price that is higher than offered, ever. This means, if any product has never been sold at a price that is higher than the discounted price, then it is just a tactic and not true or ethical.

For example, if a product, let's say an online home-study program, is offered for $2000 as the list price. The owner offers a discount of $1000 (50% off) for everyone, then, it is a 'hype' tactic. If nobody has paid the full price for the product, it means the retail price is artificially inflated and a discount is applied just to make more sales.

Fear of losing something is a more powerful psychological trigger than the pleasure of gaining something. So, marketers use this 'hype' tactic into tricking people to buy soon and buy more than they need.

To say that a discount is genuine, it must be proved that the product has already been sold at a higher price either in the past or will definitely be sold at a higher price in the near, verifiable future, like in case of 'introductory-discounts'.

Large corporations often use discounts or coupons to get access into a new market, launch a new product or claim more market share for their products or services.

When I was in school, I remember this new newspaper that started. That was the time when real newspapers were distributed to all homes, early in the morning. This new company didn't have any market share in the region. So, they started a campaign to go to every home in the town and offered a free copy of their newspaper for 2 full months. That's a 100% discount for 2 consecutive months, to try their product. It worked like a charm. If they had tried to ask their buyers to switch to their newspaper, they would have failed miserably. They offered a deep discount and took away all the risks of buying their product. Within no time, the new newspaper's market share went from zero to 75%. Within months, all other local newspapers were out of business.

So, offering discounts is not new. Sometimes, it is genuine and most of the times, especially in the Internet Marketing world, it isn't. If something is offered at a discounted price, make sure to find out the actual price or the real price of the product before you feel good about the discount.

THE TRUTH ABOUT OUTSOURCING

There is a lot of confusion on exactly how the outsourcing model works, especially in the Internet Marketing industry.

Let me clear them up for you. I know this because we have fulfilled IM related services to hundreds of marketing companies all over the world.

Outsourcing isn't a bad idea, after all. If implemented correctly, it can save money or time or both and at the same time, provide access to remote resources that were unavailable earlier. It can bring in talent and access to skills from anywhere in the world.

With the wrong hands – unethical marketers, it can become disastrous. Instead of driving the costs down, it may lead to getting short changed in terms of quality or quantity or both.

Especially in the online marketing and SEO industry, there are very few players that have their own staff for rendering services. Most have found someone in a developing country to fulfil. And, unfortunately, most marketers do not do their due-diligence to find the right fulfilment partner or they go for the cheapest service provider.

You get what you pay for. That's what happens in this case too. Marketers charge premium prices from their clients and pass on the work on 'white-label' to their fulfilment partners in a remote corner of the world. They pay them peanuts and everybody knows what they get for peanuts – monkeys!

In such cases, there are two winners and a loser. The fulfilment partner gets a small piece of the deal but that's good money because a dollar goes a long way in a developing country. They are happy. The marketer who makes the sale gobbles up the biggest chunk and wins too. The biggest loser is the chap who avails the services from such marketers. They pay top dollars thinking they are supporting a local business while they are getting cheap stuff from an untrained service provider in a different country.

They could have saved all the money by directly going to the actual service provider because technology today makes it possible to do business anywhere in the world. Alternatively, they could have paid top-dollars and got premium services for every penny they paid, by dealing with a legitimate and ethical service provider, no matter where they are located.

At infoYOGIS, a big part of our revenue used to come from fulfilling Internet Marketing services to others companies. I have seen this happen many times in the past. The marketer or a self-proclaimed GURU would first contact us, make connection, promise bulk orders and get us to sign a contract for ultra-low prices. Then he would go back and build a business around this contract, crank up the prices to 8 to 10 times, add nothing in value for the increased price and sell our services at a premium price. It is the same stuff we used to sell on our website but 10 times expensive. Today, with our presence in the market and offices worldwide, our services are available to our clients directly, at reasonable prices and world-class quality.

FREE... REALLY!?

The word FREE is one of most used and abused word in the history of marketing. The word 'free' is powerful and a psychological hot button that is used by marketers for centuries. It also connects people to the word 'freedom' that resonates with human beings being free to control or obligation or will of another, like in political freedom.

Giving something away for free makes sense only if that 'something' is of value to the recipient. Most marketers do not get this correctly and offer useless stuff that nobody wants or they go a step further and implement this half-baked knowledge into their client's business as well.

Businesses and individuals hire marketers or marketing companies because they think they are experts in their field and let these experts manage their online marketing activities. Very dangerous. Not recommended at all. Marketing or branding is an important part of any individual or a business and must be dealt by trained professionals only. Just like you go to a doctor when your body needs surgery… you go to an architect to construct buildings… Similarly, you need a real and experienced marketing expert to take care of your online marketing needs.

If someone offers you anything for free or if YOU are offering anything for free on your website, it is time to pause and look whether the free stuff offered is useful and valuable. Does it help? Does it make any sense? If yes, continue. Otherwise, stop the nonsense and think of offering something else for free, genuinely.

There are many things that marketers offer for free including free reports, eBooks, software, free bonuses for buying the products they recommend and so on. It is not wrong to offer something for free. However, just make sure the value still exists even though the price is set to zero.

For example, at infoYOGIS, we offer a free online business assessment for people who need online marketing help. This report is actually put together by a team of people. They spend hours to research and collate the data and put together a report that is full of useful content that the recipient can actually use in their business.

I also do regular Google Hangouts on Air and broadcast my talk all over the world on topics like "Stardom Strategies", for example. These are strictly "no-sales" webinars. There won't be anything to offer at the end of these webinars. They are full of valuable content and offered for free. The only purpose of such events is to educate my audience. Teach them, train them and to an extent, entertain them. That's all. My members LOVE those hangouts because they get valuable information that they can use in their lives right away!

The best way to offer something for free is to create a product (or a service), fix a price, sell a few copies and THEN offer it for free. That's a really free offer.

HYPE TRIGGERS

Here are some words that I call as hype-triggers. When I see those words or phrases, my hype-guard goes up. Unscrupulous marketers and scammers use these heavily to push their stuff. When you see such words in emails, offers and announcements, pause for a moment and do a thorough reality-check before proceeding.

Expert – used widely. I wonder how anyone can become an expert in days while people who have devoted their lifetime or decades of their life still don't consider themselves as experts!

Secret – Ah... the classic hype trigger word. Today, everyone seems to have a secret. Watch out for this. Making a lot of rounds, especially in the Internet Marketing circles.

Traffic – Essentially means website traffic. Unethical marketers are selling packages that promises website visitors and delivering crap.

First Page Rankings – Another classic hype. Nobody can promise first page rankings without first evaluating the keywords. Even then, if anyone offers first-page rankings, look with suspicion.

More Hype Triggers – Other common marketing hype trigger words include solution, push-button effort, all the touch of a button, backdoor entry (yes, used to trick people into believing there are such hidden methods for otherwise hard strategies), confidential report, winning or lottery related, free giveaways etc. Feel free to add to this list, other hype-triggers that you come across.

Hell, there are no rules here - we're trying to accomplish something.

— Thomas A. Edison

Chapter Four

Online Marketing
What Works and What Doesn't?

If you have read this book from the beginning or at least the last chapter, you have already understood that Internet Marketing is all about traffic and everyone and their DOG is a SEO consultant. Being the owner of Asia's LARGEST Internet Marketing Agency and working in this industry for more than decade (as of writing this book), I'd like to focus your attention on some of the old-world strategies that aren't effective today and what you need to do instead.

My job is to educate my audience and steer them away from unethical marketing practices that are still selling out-dated stuff to customers seeking online marketing help.

Let's begin.

OLD WORLD STRATEGY	NEW WORLD STRATEGY
FOCUS ON SEO =>	BRANDING/REPUTATION

In the OLD WORLD, the focus was on SEO or search engine optimization. In the NEW WORLD, It is BRANDING and REPUTATION.

Old-world SEO strategies like distributing articles, spinning them into hundreds of versions and spamming article directories, sending out tasteless press releases that nobody reads, building irrelevant links and other cheap-strategies don't work in the new world.

Today, your focus should be on creating or building your BRAND. Increasing your reputation online. Strengthening the TRUST you have with your audience. Whether you like it or not, people nowadays, always research about you online, BEFORE they deal with you.

OLD WORLD STRATEGY	NEW WORLD STRATEGY
ADVERTISING =>	ENGAGE AUDIENCE

ADVERTISING was something that used to work in the old days. Online advertising vehicles like banners, pay-per-click or PPC and even those annoying flash ads and disrupting overlay video ads used to work well. But not anymore. Tell me… how many times have YOU, personally, clicked a sponsored ad that appears on the right sidebar on Google?

Most people who go to search engines are looking for FREE information, seeking knowledge and trying to get some facts…. NOT looking for products to buy, with their wallets open.

In the NEW WORLD, your focus should be on…. ENGAGING YOUR AUDIENCE. In the new world, teaching is selling. Engage your audience with valuable information, insights and your perspectives. People don't like to be sold, even though they love buying. Start engaging conversations with your audience… in multiple formats like text, images, video, audio, webinars and hangouts… like the one you are watching right now.

Let's move on...

OLD WORLD STRATEGY	NEW WORLD STRATEGY
PROMOTIONS => CAMPAIGNS	

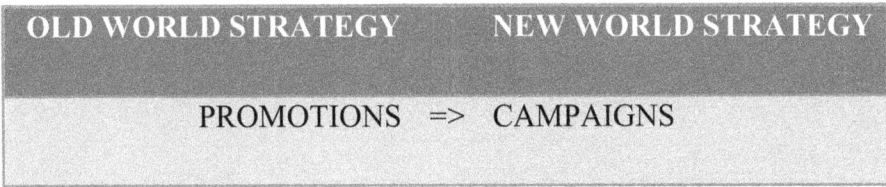

The next OLD WORLD strategy that needs to be replaced is... PROMOTION. During the early days of online marketing, the buzzword was promotion. You used to PROMOTE your marketing messages, you also worked toward getting affiliates and JV partners to PROMOTE as well. Several years ago, an email promotion could bring in the required sales.

In the new world, promotions should be replaced with CAMPAIGNS. Yes... and the differences between a promotion and a campaign are...

- Promotions are one-time events whereas Campaigns are a series of events.
- Promotions are general, mass advertising while Campaigns are strategically crafted marketing messages for specific audience.
- Promotions are geared towards achieving sales whereas Campaigns are geared towards building and nurturing a

following that will add a lot more to the bottom line by becoming life-long customers and your brand-ambassadors.

This leads us to the next OLD WORLD effort...

OLD WORLD STRATEGY	NEW WORLD STRATEGY
FIND NEW CLIENTS =>	DELIGHT CLIENTS

FINDING NEW CLIENTS – Well... I don't have to say much... gone are the days of finding new clients all the time. The competition is tough and it takes a lot more effort and resources to find new clients than DELIGHTING EXISTING CLIENTS. That's the new world strategy. When I consult businesses on their marketing plan, this is one of the first things I try to figure out. What are they doing to keep existing clients happy? What are they doing to increase the value for their customers? How can they sell more by providing better widgets to their established followers?

In fact, very recently, I was following a product launch. It was a software product, a highly successful one at that. There were thousands of users for that software. It worked very well and fulfilled all the promises made by the developer. And, the developer came out with a brand new version of that software. It was built from the ground-up, had the same name but totally brand-new features and incorporated the latest technology. However, during the launch, they completely ignored their existing client base – literally thousands of users who had PAID to get their earlier software. I guess almost all of them would have LOVED to get the new version and even PAY to get it. Unfortunately, the developer just ignored the existing customers and didn't even send an email announcement about the new software. Thousands of customers, including me, felt we were ignored. Pity, I must say. A well-planned pre-launch campaign could have brought in millions of dollars in revenue, even before the product hit the shelves.

Even some of the brilliant minds on the planet don't get the basic stuff right – keeping existing clients delighted.

Moving further....

The next OLD WORLD strategy is....

OLD WORLD STRATEGY	NEW WORLD STRATEGY
VARIOUS OFFERS => PRODUCT FUNNELS	

Here you go – "VARIOUS OFFERS". Yes... presenting offer upon offer is so much old-world. It goes something like this... you present an offer to your audience, some of them buy, some don't, you don't care... you come back with another offer. This goes on and on until you go broke or stop getting any response from your audience, if any are left. Remember the saying... "People do not like to be sold, even though they love to buy." In other words, everybody loves shopping... but nobody loves to get sold.

Instead of presenting different offers, focus on building "PRODUCT FUNNELS". Arrange your offers from least to most – in terms of quality, time, effort, fee, importance or value and make it easy for your customers to graduate from one level to the next. For example, by arranging your offers into least expensive to most expensive, you are building a FUNNEL or a PIPELINE that will enable your prospects to try your stuff with minimal resources, get the value, reap the benefits and take up on your next level, paying the additional fee. Makes sense, isn't it?

Here comes a real killer – this is one of the MOST active viruses that I'm going after in the IM industry –

OLD WORLD STRATEGY	NEW WORLD STRATEGY
FIRST PAGE RANKINGS =>	FOCUS ON FOLLOWERS

FIRST PAGE RANKINGS. Many GURUs and IM Companies are promising their clients to get them on the first page of Google and ripping them off royally, in the mean time. We have discussed this bane at the start of this hangout. It is one of the ugly faces of the IM industry and an unethical practice that needs to be rooted out completely.

So, what do you need to do?

In the new world, you must focus on FOLLOWERS instead of going after first page rankings. By putting in efforts to build a fan following will definitely give you better results than appearing in the first page of search results for keywords that no one is searching for.

If given a choice to choose between first page rankings for a bunch of keywords that may or may not have searches and a bunch of followers that admire your message, what would you choose?

If you said, followers, you are right on, my friend.

This brings us to the last MARKETING FALLACY that is definitely old world AND making a lot of rounds recently… I will tell you why, in a moment and that is…

OLD WORLD STRATEGY	NEW WORLD STRATEGY
MUST HAVE K/S/A =>	HAVE ACCESS TO K/S/A

The fallacy of having K..S..A..

Knowledge, Skills and Abilities.

Using this concept, many self proclaimed GURUs have been minting a lot of money by launching courses, educational programs and home study material, in the name of online marketing training.

Unless you want to become an online marketer, you don't need to learn about online marketing. In fact, I too have launched my own home study course. And, that was to teach people on how to start their OWN Internet Marketing Agency. This is not for my clients who wanted us to do their online marketing for them.

In the new world, all you need is ACCESS to Knowledge, Skills and Abilities. You don't need another home study course or an expensive seminar to learn about Internet Marketing. You need someone who is an expert on that topic.

Who is the most successful person in your industry? Unless you are trying to become an online marketer, do you think that person knows everything about online marketing? Hell.. no! What makes the person successful is not their online marketing skills… it is the value that the person is providing to his or her audience. Most often than not, they have access to other people who have K..S..A.

For example, let's say, the most successful author is extremely good at her topic but she doesn't design her own graphics, websites, book covers or cares to run her marketing campaigns. What makes her successful is the value she gives to her audience and other experts handle the rest.

Here's the full list of old-world and new-world strategies at a glance.

OLD WORLD STRATEGY	NEW WORLD STRATEGY
FOCUS ON SEO =>	BRANDING/REPUTATION
ADVERTISING =>	ENGAGE AUDIENCE
PROMOTIONS =>	CAMPAIGNS
FIND NEW CLIENTS =>	DELIGHT CLIENTS
VARIOUS OFFERS =>	PRODUCT FUNNELS
FIRST PAGE RANNKINGS =>	FOCUS ON FOLLOWERS
MUST HAVE K/S/A =>	GET ACCESS TO K/S/A

Experience is not what happens to you;
it's what you do with what happens to you.

— Aldous Huxley

Chapter Five

Time To Stop

In today's digital world, spreading your message on the
Internet is the most effective way. Internet marketing is a medium
that is all-pervasive and helps you reach audiences far and wide. It is
also the fastest way to reach. However, it is time to STOP whatever
you are doing in the name of Internet Marketing and take a closer
look and figure out whether the current strategies are working or
whether they belong to the old-world, doing more damage than help.

My sole purpose of this book is to educate you and steer you
away from ineffective marketing methods and save you from
unethical marketers who may still be using obsolete strategies on
your business.

Here are some really bad marketing techniques from the OLD-WORLD, that you MUST stop doing, right now.

Link Building

You don't need to actually build links. If your message is engaging, it will happen automatically – which is the best way to get links. Stop BUYING links, especially from bad neighborhoods. There are services that sell links. Some marketers and marketing companies offer packaged services and link building is a big part of such packages. Stay away from such practices. They do more harm than help. Link building should happen naturally and on its own. That's what Google likes. It is best when your audience, fans and followers start sharing your content by linking to your content from other websites, social networks and blogs.

Article Distribution

Before you start distributing articles, pause and answer the question "Who cares?" Stop getting articles written by some unknown newbie in a corner of the world that knows nothing about your topic… and YOU putting YOUR name to that crap that gets distributed all over the Internet! It will hurt you and your reputation in the long run. If you really care about your audience, YOU write your own articles. You don't need to be a great writer. You only need to know your stuff – that's it. If you know your stuff, write notes and take the help of a professional editor to finish it up for you. THAT'S having access to KSA. Obama doesn't write his own articles or speeches. He makes points and professional writers polish those points up and make them into a great article or an engaging speech.

Gone are the days when you could hire a virtual assistant, give her a few keywords and ask her to write articles with your keywords stuffed into them strategically and then send them over all those 'article-distribution networks'. The same article goes to hundreds of websites and the worst thing about this is, nobody reads those articles.

Marketing companies and SEO consultants know that as well. However, the idea was to get as many 'keyword' links back to the primary website as possible so that Google will see that as a reason to rank the primary website higher.

Google changed their algorithm overnight and rendered this 'previously working' strategy futile. So if you are doing this or if your marketing service provider is doing this as part of a monthly-package, stop this as soon as possible.

And, the next one is… one of the most abused techniques in the IM industry…

Press Releases

Stop releasing unwanted news that nobody reads. Just like some joker writing articles about topics that they don't have a clue about, so-called PR experts are churning out Press Releases... creating them from thin air and circulating them all over the Internet. If you have hired someone to write and distribute press releases, STOP wasting electrons. Stop adding to the woes of information-overload.

Press Releases make sense and work well ONLY if the story is newsworthy. If you have anything that could be breaking news in your industry, THEN you definitely need a press release. And, an experienced media professional, not an amateur PR writer, should prepare that piece. Newspapers around the world are inundated with hundreds of thousands of press releases every day. Not all of them get into the media. So, if you want to use Press Releases as a marketing strategy, use it diligently and let an experienced and trained professional do it for you.

The objective of a press release should be to get the attention of real newspapers and magazines and get them printed or added to their news websites, not just to get into the database of millions of other press stories that nobody picks up or reads.

TIP: I suggest identifying a specific newspaper or an industry magazine and pitch your article to the editor in charge for your targeted section. This works way better than sending a press release and waiting to see if it gets picked up. Most often, it won't make it. Directly interacting with the editors or journalists gets the job done quickly and easily. Many times, they will even suggest how exactly they want your news story, in terms of length, story angle and content.

Blog Commenting

This is really awful. Long gone are the days when you hired someone to search for blog posts about your topic and sneak in your marketing message into the conversation. It used to work back THEN… now, it is called spamming and it annoys others. In fact, it does more damage than help. So, stop this, unless you are really adding value to the conversation. Blogs are very personal for people who own or manage them and it is their turf. Marketers need to show some decency when they are on other people's turf and stop annoying the blog owners, with unwanted marketing messages strewn all over the blog.

Most 'packaged' marketing services offer blog commenting as part of the program. And, they do it each and every month – annoying others!

Forum Posting

Posting and commenting on Forums is equally annoying. It used to work in the early days of online marketing. Today, just like blog commenting, they are considered as spam. The best way to use this medium is to engage your audience with useful content, instead of a source to distribute your links and marketing messages.

Forums are a great place to look out for ideas or doing surveys. There are really cool forums in every imaginable niche that can be leveraged for connecting with your audience but definitely not for distributing links or spamming the networks.

Pay Per Click

Pay Per Click or PPC is again, a debatable marketing strategy that may or may not work in your situation. There are certain industries, offers and situations where PPC may still be extremely effective. But, for most other mainstream marketing, PPC in it's current format isn't as effective as it used to be.

Especially, today, there's more competition to the same keywords and the money paid to get a click, in most cases, doesn't justify the spending at all. The same money could be spent in other marketing efforts that are more effective.

At the time of writing this book, the PPC technology is undergoing a drastic transformation. Facebook, LinkedIn, Twitter and other networks have their own PPC platforms. Some are new, some are changing. New technologies like 'video indexing' and advertising on videos are emerging. All these years, there was no way to actually "read" and index video content. Now, newer technologies are making that possible, which will eventually lead to placing ads at specific sections in a playing video. It is better to wait and see how the new technologies work in this sector before investing on campaigns.

If you are doing any of these activities like link building, article distribution and other old-world strategies to get FIRST PAGE RANKINGS, STOP them immediately.

There are new and better ways to attract the attention of your audiences that do not depend on search engines or algorithm changes. In the next chapter I will share ideas on some of these concepts.

A little more persistence, a little more effort,
and what seemed hopeless failure
may turn to glorious success.

— Elbert Hubbard

Chapter Six

New Beginnings

Thinking beyond the search engines.

Evolution is a continuous process. New beginnings bloom from where it all ended. SEO is dead and new strategies are going to replace this once famous and highly effective bunch of methodologies.

Let me introduce you to concepts for building your reputation and branding that do not depend on search engines. Let the search engines do their own business and let us focus on strategies leading to stardom.

EDUCATE

So now that I have told you what you SHOULD NOT do. Here are few things you MUST DO or FOCUS on DOING immediately. The number way to do this is by educating your audience about your topic. Start giving and then you will start getting more than you have ever imagined.

In the new world, selling is teaching. If you start teaching, you will build a fan base that appreciate what you have and ultimately will become eager to buy your offers.

One of the best results of having admirers around is the boost it gives to your confidence and self-esteem.

Stop building products for everybody on the planet. Focus on specific groups of people that you want to serve and start serving them by educating your audience.

Giving away high quality content right off the bat is not only ethical, it will also make YOU an authority in your niche.

This concept will work in every industry and situation. If you are selling products or services, it works. If you are a non-profit, it works too. If you have a message, you can propagate it by educating your audience. And, this doesn't depend on any changes beyond your control like search engine updates or the arrival of a new social network.

Every successful business and organization has adapted this principle. Look at Microsoft, Apple, Adobe – they sell more of their products because they train and educate more and more people to use their products.

Long ago, when software pirates were distributing Microsoft's products illegally, Microsoft didn't do anything. They just let the pirates do an excellent job of getting Microsoft's products into as many computers as possible. Then they started training the recipients of those software programs with certified training programs. What happened next is history. Microsoft soon became a software giant because everybody in their market started using those products.

A very brilliant entrepreneur that I admire and appreciate, my friend, Brendon Burchard chose a similar model. He came from nowhere, started giving away high quality content and soon became highly popular with an enormous fan base. Later when he launched his program, seminars and products, people not only purchased whole-heartedly, but also became his brand ambassadors. That's because he took the time to train his audience with good quality content and useful information.

I have seen the concept of EDUCATING THE AUDIENCE work across the board, from individuals to multi-national companies to non-profits to even Government organizations. They have all had exceptional returns for taking time to educate their audience.

Here are some ways you can start educating your audience.

Make Videos

Visuals in the form of pictures and sound tell a story and can deliver your message quickly and efficiently to your audience. With the latest technology, making and distributing videos is not only fast but also very inexpensive. Start educating your audience using videos. Teach simple concepts; break into sessions and answer questions on video.

Publish INFOGRAPHICS

Hire a professional designer and develop info-graphics. These are high-resolution, high-quality pictures that are often huge in size and contain useful information depicted using pictures, charts and illustrations. Info-graphics are very popular nowadays and people love to share them on social networks.

Start HANGOUTS

Hanging out with friends and partying is fun. With Google's latest technology, you can now hangout with your fans, audience and members and conduct online meetings and conferences effortlessly. All you need is a laptop (or a computer with a camera) and an

Internet connection. Webinars using Google's 'Hangouts on Air' technology has brought the once expensive LIVE BROADCASTING platform to everybody who is connected to the Internet. The possibilities are endless.

Publish a Digital Magazine

Tablet computing is on the rise. Millions of people are now using tablets including iPads, for browsing the Internet. High quality digital magazines can now be easily delivered to such devices. New publishing platforms and software available today can package content into beautifully laid out digital magazines and delivered to subscribers anywhere in the world. This is a great new way to educate your audience because people love to read magazines today, instead of eBooks. Magazines can be made interesting by embedding visuals, audio and video. It can also include live links and interactive media. This is indeed a great tool to educate AND entertain your audience at the same time.

Author a Book

Extremely easy to use self-publishing technologies have paved way for the new literary-age. Writing and publishing books is no more the domain of the elite and the well informed. Today, anyone can write his or her own book and there is not even a need to find a publisher. It can be published in no time. Can be digitally delivered via e-publishing platforms like Amazon's Kindle. A book full of high-quality and useful content is a great way to educate your audience. It will give the author an authority status.

GO MOBILE

In order to take advantage of the new strategies it is important first to understand the trends and study the facts.

10.3 Million Terabytes

The amount of mobile data traffic that will occur per month by 2017, according to recent research from iGR.

48%

The amount of 18-24 year old who believe text messaging is just as meaningful as an actual conversation with the person on the phone, according to a Tyntec and Mobile Groove study, which found that the app developers are relying more on SMS to engage users and further monetize their apps.

92%

Consumers who indicated they prefer to shop and make purchases on websites that display product price in their local currency (source: E4X)

41%

The portion of all emails that were opened on a mobile device (phone and/or tablets) in the second half of 2012. (Source: Knotice Mobile Email Opens report for H2 2012)

60%

The fraction of brand owners who freely admitted to offering their online users only an average or below-average digital experience, according to a recent WhatUsersDo global research survey.

There is one common inference from all these facts – Go Mobile. Countless other research studies have clearly established that 'mobilizing' is the way to go.

If you haven't already, convert your website to mobile platforms. Make sure your website looks good on various mobiles devices, including iPhone, iPad, Android and other tablet devices.

If you are using Wordpress as the CMS for your website, making it available for both desktop and mobile users is easy. Find a suitable Wordpress "theme" and make sure it is RESPONSIVE. A responsive theme is an approach to web development that allows a website to break itself down smoothly across multiple monitor sizes, screen resolutions, and platforms, be it a computer, tablet or a mobile device. It allows the developer to create a site that is optimized for each platform, both in navigation, readability and load time.

You can also use a dedicated mobile platform for keeping the content on your desktop website and mobile version, separate. There are many such platforms that are intuitive and easy to use, such as, Dudamobile and Wompmobile.

The two major benefits of having a mobile-ready website are:

1.   Visibility

2.   Ease-of-use

Your mobile website can get more attention, leading to action, because more and more people are accessing the Internet on their mobile devices. Traditional desktop websites look terrible on mobiles and turns off visitors whereas a properly formatted mobile website is more likely to retain the attention of your visitors for a longer time.

By building a mobile version of your website and serving it automatically, you will be making it easier for your visitors to get your message. Mobiles and tablets do not have a keyboard and most interaction is visual.

Some key differentiators of a mobile website include "Click to Call", a feature that allows your mobile website users to tap a button on their phone to automatically dial your phone number; "Maps & Directions", detailed location and driving instructions directly on their device to visit; and displaying "Store Hours", to name a few.

ENGAGE

Post-SEO, it is the era of engaging your audience. Gone are the days of vying for traffic. Website visitors are inundated with information overload and their attention span is getting lower and lower.

If you really want to build your brand and business in the new world, it is time to start engaging your audience in various ways. Just a static website or even a regularly updated blog isn't enough. The interaction should be from both the sides – you and your audience.

Integrations are happening everywhere. People can login to your website or subscribe to your newsletter automatically, using social logins. Users of Gmail, Facebook and other social media can use the same credential to create logins on your website as well, eliminating the need to remember another username and password. By enabling social login on email opt-ins, the number of subscribers will go up because it removes a hassle and the details are already filled in.

Integration technology also allows your audience to interact on your website using other platforms. For example, you can have Facebook comments integrated into any page on your website. Or, you can even go a step further and signup for a service called "LiveFYRE" and integrate various commenting platforms into one, easily-manageable comment-box on ANY page of your website. At the time of writing this book, Livefyre's commenting system was free to signup.

It is time to integrate offline and online seamlessly. Here are 5 ways to integrate and engage your prospects:

- On-the-spot Reviews
- Video Testimonials
- Contests and Surveys
- Incentivized 'Check-Ins'
- Live Broadcasts

On-the-spot reviews are used mainly by offline businesses. They ask their customers, clients and store visitors to write a short review right after they are served. For example, a tour operator can ask their customer to write a short online review about the tour, right after the tour ends. Customers are delighted and in a better mood to say a few words of appreciation on the spot.

Video testimonials are a great way to interact with your website visitors. Do not bury your video testimonials on the website under multiple clicks. Bring them to the front. Let people see what others are talking about you.

Contests and surveys add a lot of interactivity to websites. It also shows that you care and want your users' input. As a bonus, you will also get to know what your visitors and users are thinking. Most people won't express without asking, whether the feedback is positive or negative. Contests add a lot of buzz and surveys provide you with insights. Make these 2 strategies a part of your marketing plan.

Offline businesses can create a lot more buzz by incentivizing 'check-ins' to their store. Restaurants, for example, can offer an incentive, maybe in the form of a free drink or an upgrade or even a small gift... in exchange for "checking in" on various online platforms like Facebook or Foursquare.

With little modification, this can be used by online businesses and websites as well. I have personally used this strategy on my Hangouts at StardomAlliance.com. For select webinars, I give a small (but valuable) incentive, in the form of a download, for people who share the details about my webinar on social media. This is handled automatically by the website software – offering a download, setting up a condition (share details on social media), verifying whether the condition was met and serving the download link.

One of the most recent developments and a really super-cool way to engage your audience is through live webinars and hangouts. Google has paved way for conducting live broadcasts and webinars with their "Hangouts on Air" technology. Today, anyone can do webinars and live events from anywhere in the world. Unlimited people can connect and watch as well as interact with you online, all the while using Google's robust software and hardware platform. All you need is a computer with camera (or a laptop) and an Internet connection. Even modern tablets are capable of harnessing this technology.

BRAND & REPUTATION

The American Marketing Association (AMA) defines a brand as a "name, term, sign, symbol or design, or a combination of them intended to identify the goods and services of one seller or group of sellers and to differentiate them from those of other sellers".

Therefore it makes a lot of sense to understand that branding is not just about getting your target market to choose you over the competition, but it is about getting your prospects and audience to see you as the only one that provides a solution to their problems.

A strong brand is invaluable as the battle for customers, especially online, intensifies day by day. It's crucially important to spend considerable time in researching, defining, and building your brand and online reputation. After all, your brand is the source of a promise to your audience. It's a foundational piece in your marketing communication and one you do not want to be without.

Branding is not just for corporates. Everyone should build their own personal branding, especially online. People don't do businesses with other businesses, they deal with people. Whether you like it or not, almost everyone you interact with, will almost always check you out on the Internet, first. That has become the norm today.

A well thought-out branding strategy is a must for individuals and businesses alike. And, this is not dependent on external factors like search engines or social media.

CORE MESSAGING

What is your message to the world?

Why should people pay attention to you?

You can greatly increase the effectiveness of your message and spread it far and wide, by creating a "core-message video". Many people do not have a professionally made sizzle video. Some have, but they bore their visitors with lengthy, amateurish, blurry videos with barely audible sound. Most often the videos are parts of their lengthy presentations.

What's needed is a short, sizzle video that talks directly about the core message. Something similar to an elevator speech, on video. Videos that are slick and professionally rendered, giving solid reasons why visitors should stay on the website or listen to you. When visitors are engaged with such content, they are more likely to stay longer.

RESPONSIBLE SOCIAL POSTING

Social media has paved way for 2-way interactions and enabled people to develop and nurture their own fan following. It is a great tool that needs to be used responsibly.

You many times have you seen people posting all sorts of nonsense on social networks like, personal funny pictures, cat humping another cat, bizarre and scary pictures and so on. It is okay for personal sharing between friends. When it comes to building your brand, strengthening your reputation online and becoming an authority on your topic, you must exercise great care and responsibility on what you post on social networks.

By cutting out crap and regularly posting useful content for your followers, you will soon become one of the most sought-after authorities on the topic. People will start interacting, asking questions, commenting on posts and even liking your content as soon as you post.

By positioning yourself as an authority on the topic, using the new-world strategies that do not depend on SEO, search engines or any other phenomena, you will soon become the go-to person in your niche.

Do what you love to do and give it your very best.
Whether it's business or baseball, or the theater, or any field.
If you don't love what you're doing and you can't give it
your best, get out of it. Life is too short.
You'll be an old man before you know it.

— Elbert Hubbard

Chapter Seven

Conclusion

With due respects to the "SEO Club" that propelled millions of websites and spawned itself into a huge, world-wide industry, it is time to lay it to rest and move on.

When you see the evolution of mankind, the time it takes for a huge leap, is getting smaller and smaller over time. It took millenniums for the mankind to figure out fire, farming and clothing. It took centuries to master art, medicine and engineering. It took just decades to conquer the land, water and air. After the industrial revolution and the jet-age, we are well past the information era.

This evolutionary and transformational process is continuous and will be always happening. Similarly, marketing too has come a long way. In the digital world, marketing has new meanings and new definitions.

Strategies that worked earlier have lost their effectiveness. Some have even transformed into foes from friends. The Internet users are transforming too. They are more intelligent than ever, more exposed to other messages and can now choose how they want to spend their time on the Internet.

SEO was always a moving target. The industry couldn't cope with the swiftness of the changes in technology. Just a few months back, it would cost hundreds of dollars and special software and training to conduct webinars whereas today, it is free, easy and accessible to everyone.

Marketing companies, consultants and agencies have to figure out new ways to spread the message of their customers. And more importantly, stop using ineffective and unethical marketing practices on unsuspecting customers.

With the right marketing strategies that do not depend on external factors, you will be able to reach your target audience quickly, efficiently and using the fastest available avenues than you can imagine.

The Speaking Tree (www.TheSpeakingTree.org)
A Movement Against Unethical Marketing

After seeing all these transformation first hand, after running my own IM agency for nearly 10 years and being in this industry for over a decade, I saw unethical marketing all over the place. Marketers scamming other people with their new 'secret', new training programs, seminars, coaching program and even mastermind circles costing over $50000.

By being an insider, I could clearly see the manipulations going on. Unethical marketers were playing with the psychology of their prospects with artificially created scarcity, urgency and the need to buy their products or services.

At first, I ignored such practices, thinking they are just small incidents that happen in any industry for that matter. Later, I started seeing more and more of these totally unethical and unjust practices by even trusted Gurus online. Finally, I thought it is "enough" when such unethical marketers started packaging and selling their "training" programs in the name of marketing!

That's when that thought of starting a movement against unethical marketing practices came to my mind, resulting in the founding of "The Speaking Tree". At www.TheSpeakingTree.org, my sole purpose is to alert people, help them in identifying marketing hype, show them the reality, steer them away from unethical marketing and GUIDE them into achieving stardom in their chosen fields.

I urge all users and recipients of online marketing services to join and support this movement. With collective wisdom, interaction and exchange of ideas, we can save hundreds or even thousands of people from getting victimized by unethical marketing practices.

All the content on the website – TheSpeakingTree.org will always be free of charge or obligations.

Acknowledgements

It is impossible to thank everyone who has helped me in arriving at this moment in my life.

I owe it to all those amazing teachers, from elementary school to high school, college and the University.

To Mom, Dad, my dear wife Poornima and two wonderful boys Vishnu and Varun – I love you all for always believing in me and letting me live my own life. Thanks for bearing with me, and my erratic working hours. Poornima, thanks for all those delicious food – I will always relish!

I would like to specially mention that everything I'm today is because of one crucial decision my mom made more than 35 years ago, when she went to admit me to school. She chose English as my first language, without which, I wouldn't be in this position today. Thank you, Amma. I wish you both were with me today.

The reason you are reading this book is because of Ranjitha, fondly known as RJ – I owe you a lot. Without you, this book would have been impossible. Thanks for all the love, care and support. Thanks for believing in me and standing by my side, at all times, especially those tough ones. Remember, I will always be there for you.

I do not know how to thank my college professor, Dr. Lakshman Rao. Sir, thanks for showering me with your blessings and teachings. I bow in respect to you and all the teachers in my life.

My utmost respect and credits for all those great people who inspired and motivated me, including but not limited to, Brendon Burchard, Tim Ferris, Seth Godin, Joe Polish, Darren Hardy, Peter Diamandis, Armand Morin and dozens of great friends, peers and thought leaders.

I also thank all of my past and present customers, clients, vendors and suppliers who believed in me and trusted me to work on your projects, marketing, business and branding. I learned a lot more serving you than during my years at college.

It is impossible to thank everyone who has helped me share my message, so I apologize to all my supporters, affiliates, fans, clients and friends not listed here. I appreciate you. Thanks too, to all our present and past teammates, employees, staff members and volunteers.

Finally, I thank YOU, the reader. Thanks for giving me this opportunity to share my voice with you. Please support me and join the movement against unethical marketing at www.TheSpeakingTree.org. Keep visiting and revisiting our page on Facebook and tell me how you are doing.

Go ahead and become a MEGA-STAR!

Godspeed.

About the Author

Raam Anand is the founder of infoYOGIS, Asia's LARGEST Internet Marketing agency. He is also the founder of Stardom Alliance, which helps people achieve stardom and become one of the most sought-after authorities in their fields. Raam started "TheSpeakingTree.org" - a movement against unethical marketing.

Raam was involved in systems programming to some of the leading banks and financial institutions in core areas like online banking, ATM interface, asset management, online transaction processing, inter-branch networking and so on.

Since 1992, Raam has served in leading positions like Technical Director of PSL, Managing Director of Tempus Data Services, CEO of infoYOGIS, besides being an active adviser to several leading financial institutions and marketing companies.

Raam stepped into Internet Marketing in the year 2001 and since then, he has published several highly successful software programs and products. His home study course - "Site Launch System" received a lot of praise and started a new market in the industry that many other people followed. His next training program "AgencyRiches" was responsible for helping many of his students to start and run their own profitable IM agencies.

Raam started his own Internet Marketing agency in 2006 called infoYOGIS. Under his leadership and vision, this company soon grew from a 1-man operation to a 100+ people organization in 3 years and went on to become the LARGEST Internet Marketing Agency in Asia.

Raam has more than a decade of experience in the IM industry and is one of the pioneers of online marketing. He has toured the world several times, visited more than 15 countries and speaks often at seminars and conferences all over the world. He also conducts workshops, boot camps and mastermind sessions. As the CEO of infoYOGIS, he also provides consulting services for large companies throughout the world.

Other than being a sought-after coach, thoughtful trainer and a well-known business leader who is ardently followed and admired by his students, Raam is also serving as the managing trustee of a non-profit institution, engaged in charity, education and research.

Get more details, additional training, download and access his videos by visiting Raam Anand's personal website at www.RaamAnand.com

www.ingramcontent.com/pod-product-compliance
Lightning Source LLC
Chambersburg PA
CBHW032014190326
41520CB00007B/466

* 9 7 8 0 6 1 5 8 7 1 3 4 9 *